LIFE UNDERGROUND

TUNNEL INTO A WORLD OF WILDLIFE

ILLUSTRATED BY
RICHARD ORR

WRITTEN BY
JOHN WOODWARD

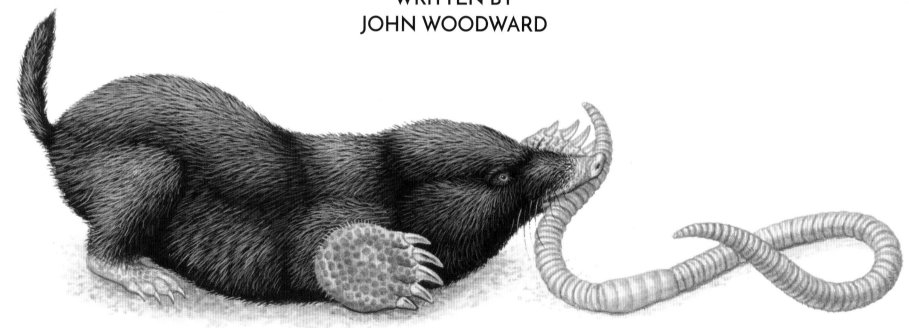

DK LONDON
Senior Editor Carron Brown
Project Art Editor Kit Lane
Designer Chrissy Checketts
Editorial Assistant Binta Jallow
Senior US Editor Kayla Dugger
Production Editor Andy Hilliard
Senior Production Controller Poppy David
Jacket Designer Stephanie Cheng Hui Tan
Jacket Design Development Manager Sophia MTT
Cartographer Simon Mumford
Managing Editor Francesca Baines
Managing Art Editor Philip Letsu
Publisher Andrew Macintyre
Associate Publishing Director Liz Wheeler
Art Director Karen Self
Publishing Director Jonathan Metcalf

DK DELHI
Senior Jackets Coordinator Priyanka Sharma Saddi
DTP Designer Rakesh Kumar
Picture Research Administrator Vagisha Pushp

First American Edition,1997,
published as *The Burrow Book*
This American Edition, 2023
Published in the United States by DK Publishing
1745 Broadway, 20th Floor, New York, NY 10019

Copyright © 2023 Dorling Kindersley Limited
DK, a Division of Penguin Random House LLC
23 24 25 26 27 10 9 8 7 6 5 4 3 2 1
001–333634–Nov/2023

A catalog record for this book
is available from the Library of Congress.
ISBN 978-0-7440-8472-6

Printed and bound in China

For the curious
www.dk.com

MIX
Paper | Supporting
responsible forestry
FSC™ C018179

This book was made with Forest
Stewardship Council™ certified
paper—one small step in DK's
commitment to a sustainable future.
For more information go to
www.dk.com/our-green-pledge

CONTENTS

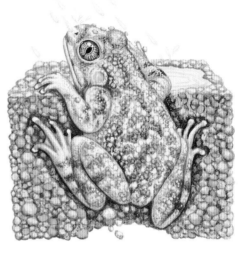

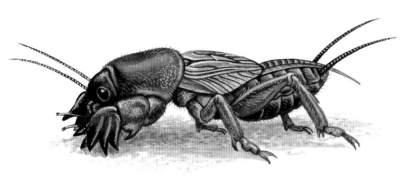

BURROW BIOMES

Animals dig burrows all over the world, but the challenges they face vary greatly depending on where they live. A tundra vole burrows beneath winter snow to escape freezing winds, but a desert jerboa hides away to avoid scorching heat. Every large-scale habitat—known as a biome—has its own types of burrowing animals, each adapted to the climate, terrain, and surrounding plant life.

KEY

- ☐ Ice
- ☐ Tundra
- ☐ Taiga
- ☐ Temperate forest
- ☐ Tropical forest
- ☐ Grassland
- ☐ Desert
- ☐ Arid scrub
- ☐ Mountain

Seashore burrowers

A community of burrowing animals lives in the sand and mud of soft tidal shores around the world. They include worms, clams, snails, crabs, and even burrowing starfish. Most are only active at high tide, with many extending feeding tubes to gather food drifting in the water above.

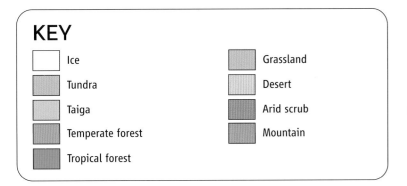

Sand gaper clam

Cockle

Baltic tellin

This burrowing starfish is eating a large sand gaper clam.

Tiny laver spire shells scour the surface for food.

The peppery furrow shell draws water in one tube and out through another.

A lugworm sucks food-rich water into its U-shaped burrow.

Sand gaper clams can burrow more than 20 inches (50 centimeters).

Tundra

In polar regions, most of the ground freezes in winter and becomes covered in snow. Animals can burrow beneath the snow to keep warm and dig into the ground when the surface thaws in summer.

Low-growing plants have the chance to flower and set seed in the short tundra summer of northern Canada.

Taiga

The vast forests of northern Eurasia and North America are called the taiga. Due to the cold climate, the ground never dries out and is often swampy, but this suits animals such as the beaver.

In fall, the foliage of deciduous trees in Quebec, Canada, glows with vivid color.

Grasslands

Regions that do not get enough rain to support woodland develop into open grassland. Many of the smaller animals burrow into the ground for shelter.

Where they have not become farmland, the North American prairies are seas of grass.

A burrower's world

This world map is color-coded to show the major biomes such as deserts, grasslands, and forests. In many regions, these natural habitats have been transformed by farming, but wild animals still live in the areas of wilderness that remain.

Mountains

High mountain ranges have harsh climates and shallow soils. But some burrowing animals make their homes among tumbled rocks, and remote river valleys can be havens for wildlife.

Many mountain landscapes, such as here in Chile, are rocky and barren, with few plants and animals.

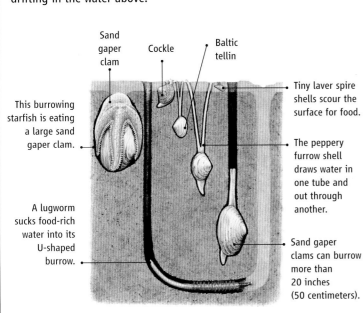

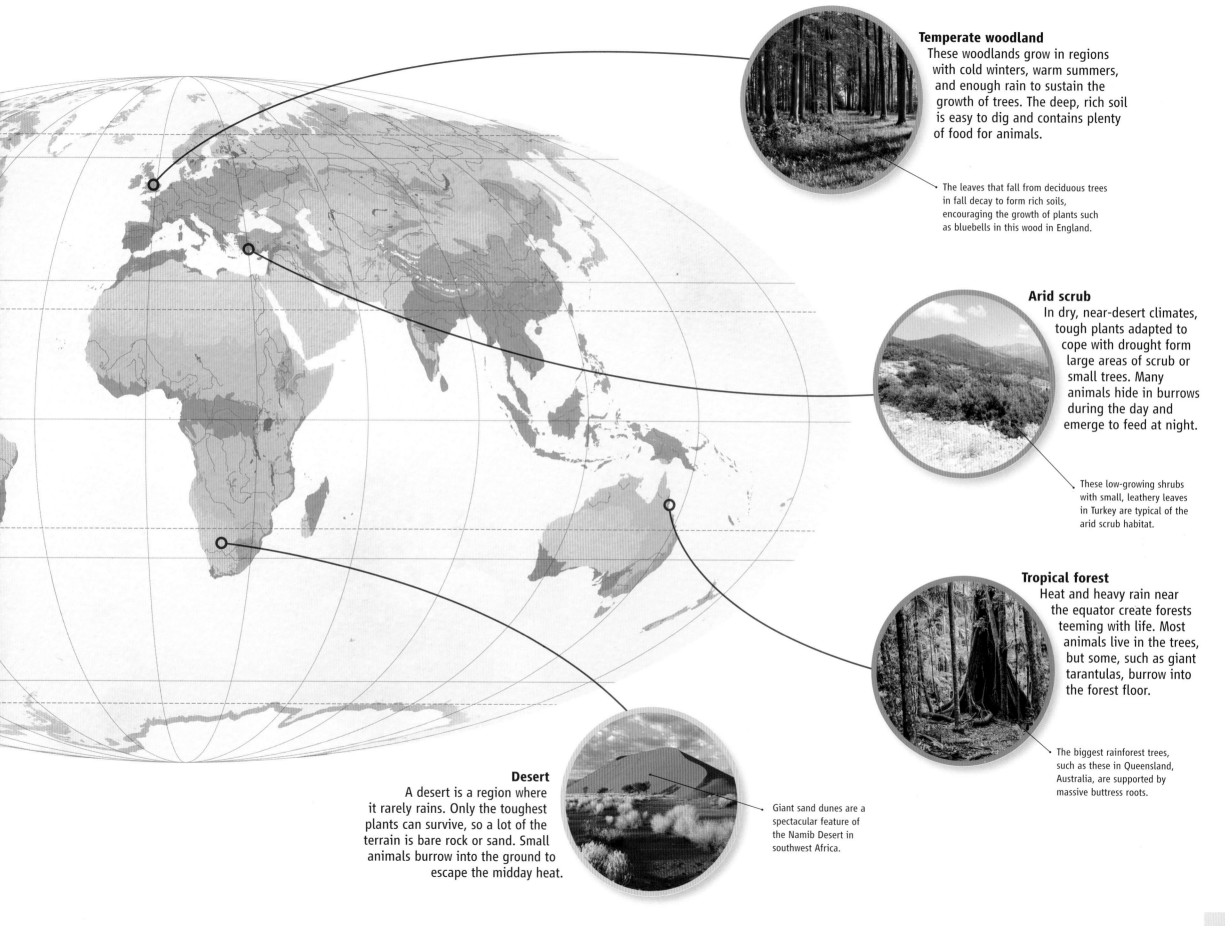

Temperate woodland
These woodlands grow in regions with cold winters, warm summers, and enough rain to sustain the growth of trees. The deep, rich soil is easy to dig and contains plenty of food for animals.

The leaves that fall from deciduous trees in fall decay to form rich soils, encouraging the growth of plants such as bluebells in this wood in England.

Arid scrub
In dry, near-desert climates, tough plants adapted to cope with drought form large areas of scrub or small trees. Many animals hide in burrows during the day and emerge to feed at night.

These low-growing shrubs with small, leathery leaves in Turkey are typical of the arid scrub habitat.

Tropical forest
Heat and heavy rain near the equator create forests teeming with life. Most animals live in the trees, but some, such as giant tarantulas, burrow into the forest floor.

The biggest rainforest trees, such as these in Queensland, Australia, are supported by massive buttress roots.

Desert
A desert is a region where it rarely rains. Only the toughest plants can survive, so a lot of the terrain is bare rock or sand. Small animals burrow into the ground to escape the midday heat.

Giant sand dunes are a spectacular feature of the Namib Desert in southwest Africa.

WHY LIVE UNDERGROUND?

Animals burrow into the ground for all kinds of reasons. A burrow makes a good home, hidden from enemies and insulated against extremes of temperature. It can be an ideal place to raise defenseless young or sleep through a long winter. But there is also food to be found in the soil, and this enables some animals to live most of their lives underground.

Hibernation

Arctic ground squirrels hibernate for more than half the year, curled up in burrows lined with leaves, grass, and animal hair. Their bodies can cool down to almost freezing point but, amazingly, they survive.

Food in the soil

Moles eat small burrowing animals, especially earthworms. They spend their lives tunneling through the soil in search of prey and rarely come to the surface.

Keeping cool

The bat-eared fox hunts by night for the termites and other insects that live on African grasslands. During the heat of the day, it retreats to a burrow where the air is cooler and stays there until the temperature drops outside.

Keeping warm

In the far north, lemmings burrow beneath the snow that covers the ground in winter. The snow acts like a thick blanket, protecting them from the freezing winds that sweep across the Arctic tundra.

Ambushing prey

A trapdoor spider lurks in its burrow under a trapdoor of silk and waits for an insect to wander by. It then flips up the trapdoor and darts out to seize its victim.

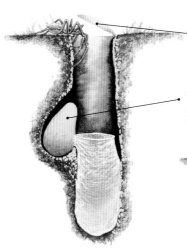

The burrow's trapdoor is made of spider silk reinforced with soil grains.

The pellet spider from Australia makes a burrow with a second door in the form of a hinged mud pellet.

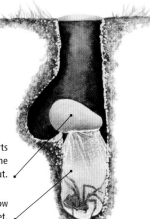

If it senses danger, the spider darts down its burrow and pulls over the pellet to keep its enemy out.

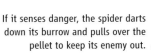

The spider uses the silk burrow lining to pull on the pellet.

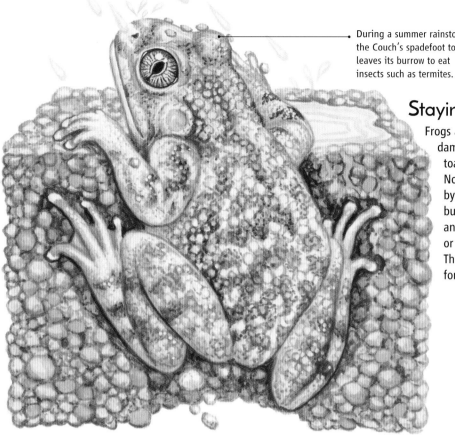

During a summer rainstorm, the Couch's spadefoot toad leaves its burrow to eat insects such as termites.

Staying wet

Frogs and toads must stay damp, but Couch's spadefoot toad lives in the deserts of North America. It survives by hiding away in a moist burrow most of the time and only feeding at night or during rare rainstorms. The toad may stay buried for up to 11 months.

Protection from predators

All kinds of small animals use burrows to hide from hungry predators. An eagle swooping overhead will make a rabbit dive into the nearest bolt-hole, and it will emerge only when it is safe.

This rabbit has a store of food in its burrow.

Looking after young

A female polar bear gives birth to her cubs in a den dug in deep snow in the Arctic. She can stay in the den for up to six months, living off her stores of fat and taking care of her cubs. A hole through the snow allows fresh air to enter the den.

Home for the whole tribe

The North American ground squirrels known as black-tailed prairie dogs excavate vast burrow networks called towns. Just one town can provide homes for thousands of animals. Above ground, prairie dog sentries bark a warning if danger is near, and the animals dive into the burrow.

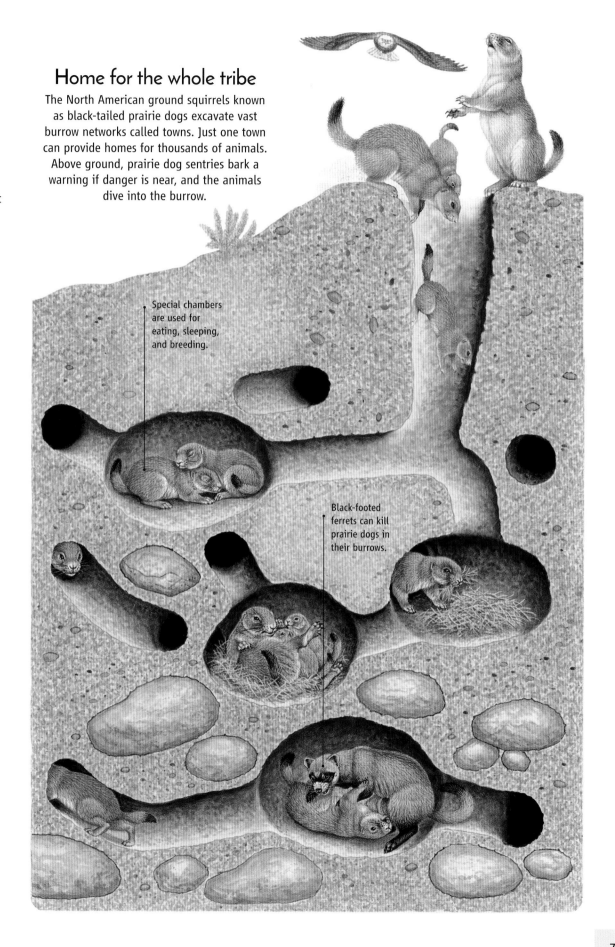

Special chambers are used for eating, sleeping, and breeding.

Black-footed ferrets can kill prairie dogs in their burrows.

WOODLAND BURROWERS

Woodlands and forests cover vast areas of land. The woodlands of temperate climates are mainly made up of broad-leaved deciduous trees that lose their leaves in winter. The fallen leaves decay to form deep soils teeming with life, which makes perfect habitats for all kinds of burrowing animals.

KEY

- Taiga
- Temperate forest
- Tropical forest
- Arid scrub

Where in the world?

Woodlands and forests grow in regions that get plenty of annual rain, although some forests have dry seasons. The driest woodland merges with arid scrub.

The mole's burrow

While birds such as this Eurasian jay forage above ground, a mole is busy digging its tunnels. These conceal it from its enemies, trap its prey, and make safe nurseries for its young.

Stoats also prey on woodland birds that feed on the ground, like this chaffinch.

In fall, jays collect acorns and bury them to eat during the winter.

Nesting chamber

Newborn baby wood mice cling to their mother's fur.

Wood mouse

Wood mice hide in burrows during the day. They store food in them and usually live there with their young.

The tail stores fat that keeps the dunnart alive if food is scarce.

Dunnart

The Australian fat-tailed dunnart is a tiny hunter that preys on smaller animals. It often builds an underground nest, which it may share with other dunnarts to keep warm.

Stoat

The long, slender body of a stoat enables it to follow prey such as voles and rabbits into their burrows and hunt them below ground.

Woodchuck

The North American woodchuck lives in a burrow consisting of long, meandering tunnels, with two to five entrances. In winter, it curls up in its burrow and hibernates for up to six months.

The mole catches earthworms that fall into its tunnels and stores them for food.

Porcupine

The crested porcupine lives in the woodlands of North Africa and Italy. It spends the day in a burrow that it digs with its claws.

KEY

1. Lesser spotted woodpecker
2. Song thrush
3. Rabbit
4. Wood pigeon

European woodland

The woodlands of northern Europe chill down in winter but burst into life in spring. As small plants flower and the tall trees grow fresh new leaves, birds such as the song thrush and wood pigeon fill the warm air with song.

1 *Lesser celandines* flower in spring on the sunlit ground beneath the bare branches of trees that lose their leaves in winter.

2 *Mole babies* sleep in nesting chambers within the underground network. Food is stored separately in different areas of the burrow.

EUROPEAN WOODLAND
Safety and warmth below ground

An amazing variety of animals live below ground in a European broad-leaved woodland. Some spend most of their lives underground. Others use burrows to raise their young or to shelter from the cold winter. Most burrowing animals have powerful legs and strong claws that are perfect for digging their homes.

12 A *parasol mushroom* is just part of a fungus network that extends deep below ground.

11 *Rabbits* dig tunnels called warrens where they live in groups. Females dig special chambers for their young.

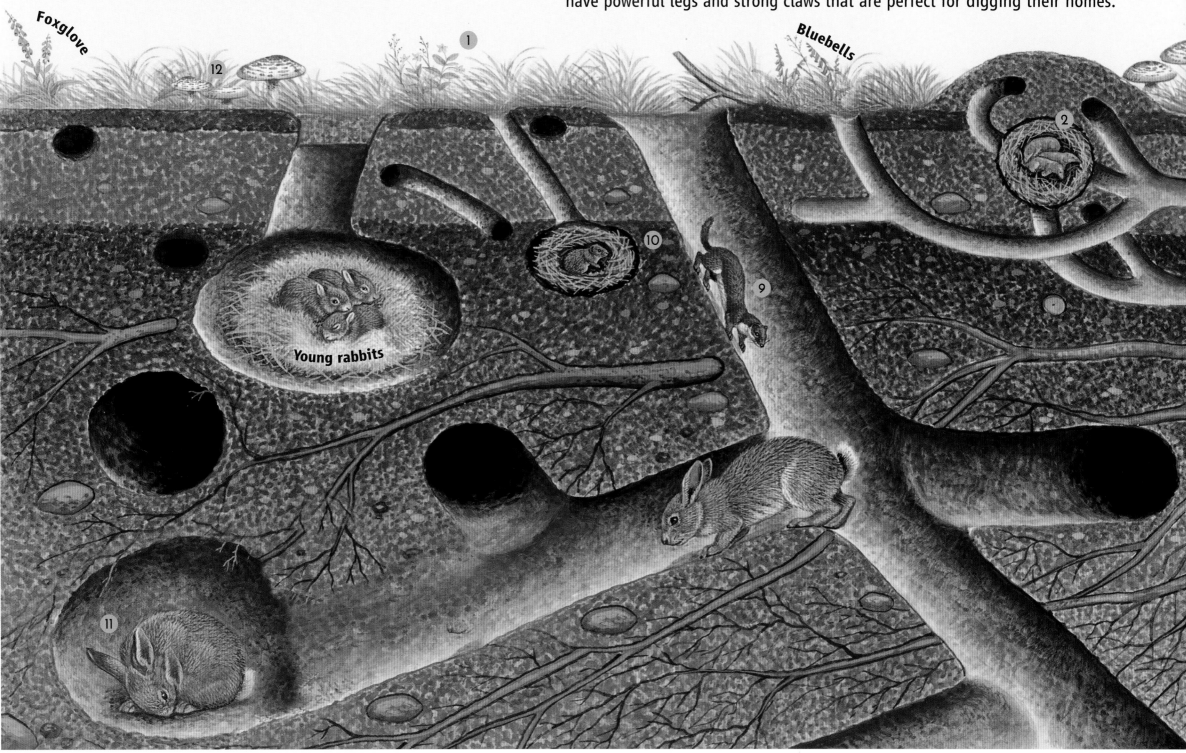

Foxglove

Bluebells

Young rabbits

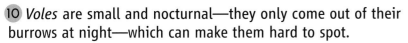

10 *Voles* are small and nocturnal—they only come out of their burrows at night—which can make them hard to spot.

9 *Weasels* hunt other animals, often entering their burrows to seize them. They also rest in the burrows when they are not hunting.

3 The *mole* digs by using its shovel-shaped feet to push the soil sideways and behind its body.

4 To give birth to her cubs, a female *red fox* digs a large burrow called an earth or moves into and enlarges an abandoned tunnel.

Red fox cubs

5 The *wood mouse* builds a nest above ground or digs a burrow, using its front feet to scape away soil.

6 *Stoats* can sneak into and make their homes in the burrows of animals they hunt.

8 *Badger* tunnels are called setts. A badger brings its bedding material ≠≠to its sett by hugging it between its neck and chin and shuffling backward.

7 In winter, the *fat dormouse* finds a tree hole or digs a burrow underground where it hibernates, sleeping through the cold months.

1 *Dung beetles* gather the dung of plant-eating animals and bury it as food for their young, helping clear up the forest floor.

2 Up to 24 inches (60 centimeters) long, the *eastern bearded dragon* preys on other animals, including insects, spiders, mice, and smaller lizards.

AUSTRALIAN SCRUB
Hidden life beneath the fallen leaves

The arid scrub of eastern Australia can cope with long periods of dry weather. The ground beneath the trees provides homes for many kinds of animals, especially insects, spiders, and burrowing reptiles.

In the cooler parts of eastern Australia, the bearded dragon spends the winter in a shallow burrow, emerging in spring to feed and find a breeding partner.

12 When a *burrow-plug gecko* dives into its burrow to hide, it uses its fat tail to block the entrance.

11 The silk lining of the *tube spider's* burrow extends above ground, anchored to a rock by silk threads.

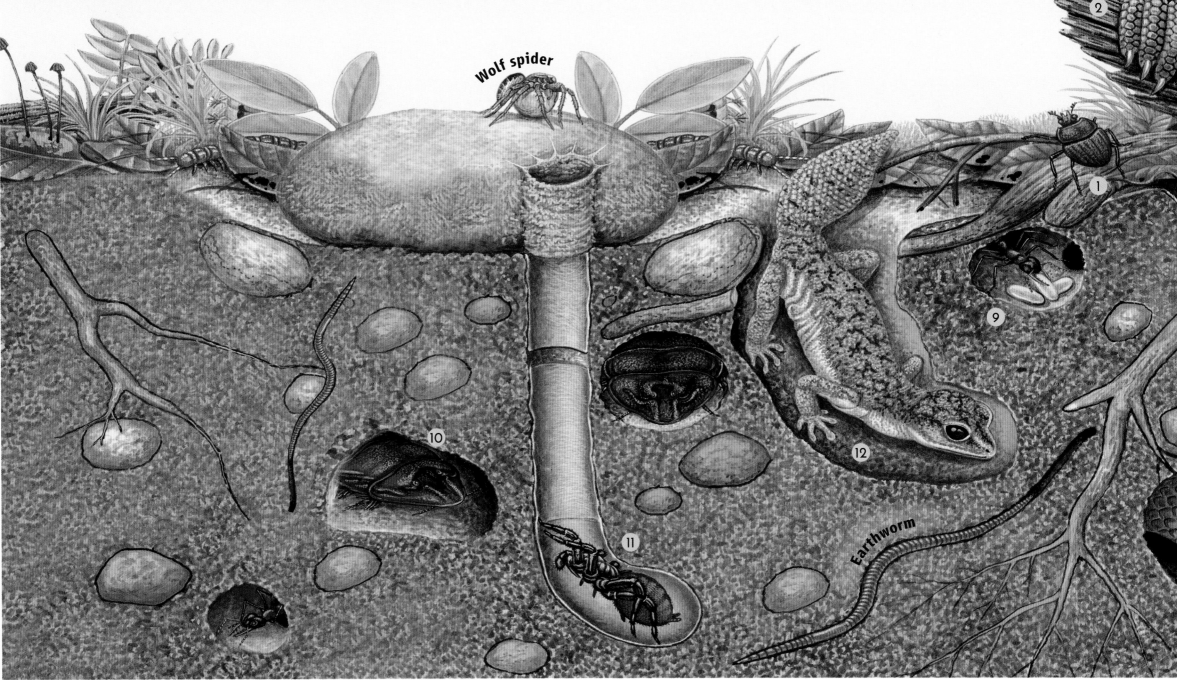

Wolf spider

Earthworm

10 Up to 3 inches (8 centimeters) long, the *rhinoceros cockroach* lives in burrows in warm, dry forests where it feeds on decomposing eucalyptus leaves.

9 Named for their fearsome jaws, *bulldog ants* also have painful stings. They form colonies of up to 300 ants, living in underground nests.

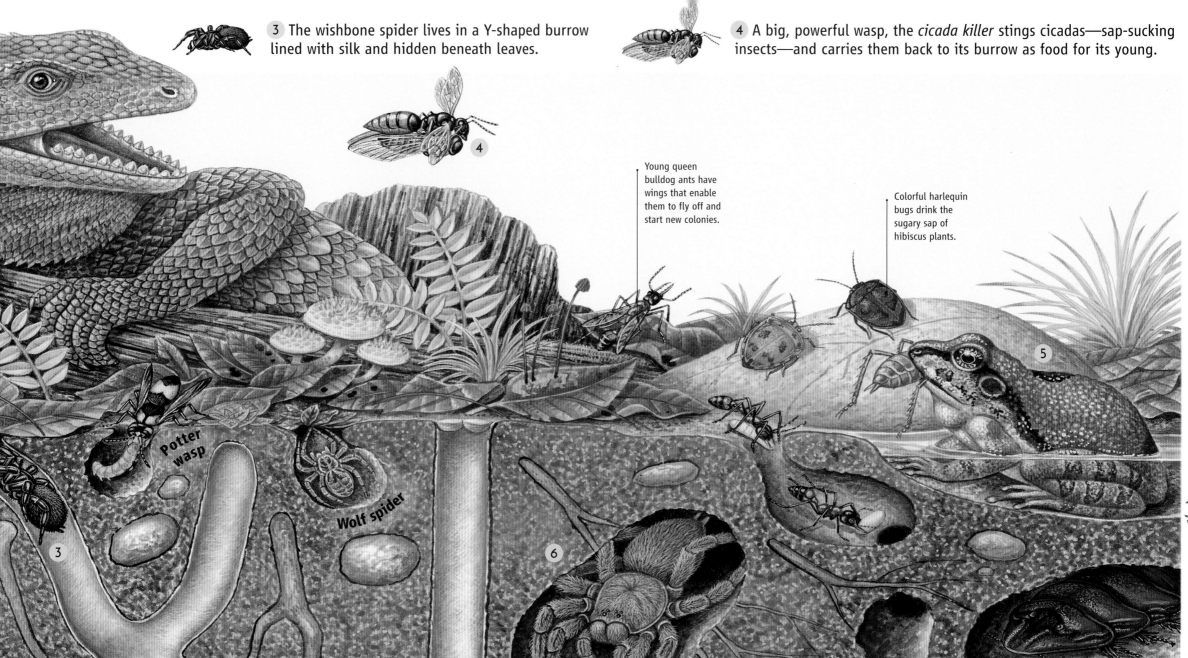

3 The wishbone spider lives in a Y-shaped burrow lined with silk and hidden beneath leaves.

4 A big, powerful wasp, the *cicada killer* stings cicadas—sap-sucking insects—and carries them back to its burrow as food for its young.

Young queen bulldog ants have wings that enable them to fly off and start new colonies.

Colorful harlequin bugs drink the sugary sap of hibiscus plants.

5 The *ornate burrowing frog* digs with its hind feet until it is completely hidden from sight.

6 The *Queensland whistling tarantula* is so called because of the sound it makes when threatened.

Potter wasp

Wolf spider

Egg cocoon

8 The *northeastern plain-nosed burrowing snake* lives in the tropical forests of Queensland. Related to cobras, it has a venomous bite.

7 A *mouse spider* uses its strong jaws to scrape away soil and make a burrow. The entrance has a hinged door made from silk and earth.

TUNDRA BURROWERS

In the far north, the snowy ground freezes during the long, cold winter, stopping trees from growing and creating the barren-looking terrain known as tundra. The bitter winter chill forces many animals to retreat underground to keep warm, but during the brief summer, the land thaws out and buzzes with life.

Where in the world?

The Arctic consists of an icy ocean surrounded by land. An ice sheet covers Greenland, but most of the Arctic landscape is tundra that can support plant and animal life.

KEY

- ☐ Ice
- ▨ Tundra

Wolverine

A heavyweight relative of weasels and polecats, the wolverine is a powerful predator. It lives all around the Arctic, in forests and on tundra, where its strong claws allow it to burrow into the frozen ground to make a den.

A wolverine can kill animals much larger than itself, including caribou.

Ermine

Also called the stoat, this slender hunter is mainly brown in summer. In the snowy Arctic, it grows a white winter coat as camouflage, hiding it from enemies and prey.

Lemmings

Notorious for their mass migrations, lemmings are relatives of voles that burrow beneath the snow in winter to keep warm, feed, and stay out of sight.

Tundra in spring

As the deep winter snow melts, flocks of geese and other migrant birds arrive to breed. Caribou and musk oxen graze the defrosted grasslands and give birth to their young.

Snow geese

Arctic skua

Musk oxen

Gray wolf

Arctic hare

Caribou

Arctic ground squirrel

Gray wolf

Arctic fox

Ermine

Brown lemming

Tundra winter scene

Life is tough for big animals such as caribou
when winter clamps down on the tundra.
Many retreat to forests, but smaller animals
can hide away beneath the snow.

Caribou

1 *Brown lemmings* feed on the grass and other plants growing beneath the snow, forming burrowlike runs through the snow itself.

2 A burrow dug into a snowdrift makes a good temporary den for a *wolverine* and her two kits, which are just a few weeks old.

CANADIAN TUNDRA
Finding shelter beneath the snow

The territory of Nunavut in northern Canada is a land of ice, snow, and treeless tundra. Most of the smaller animals that live here survive the harsh climate by burrowing beneath the snow, which insulates them from the freezing winds that sweep across the open landscape, even in spring.

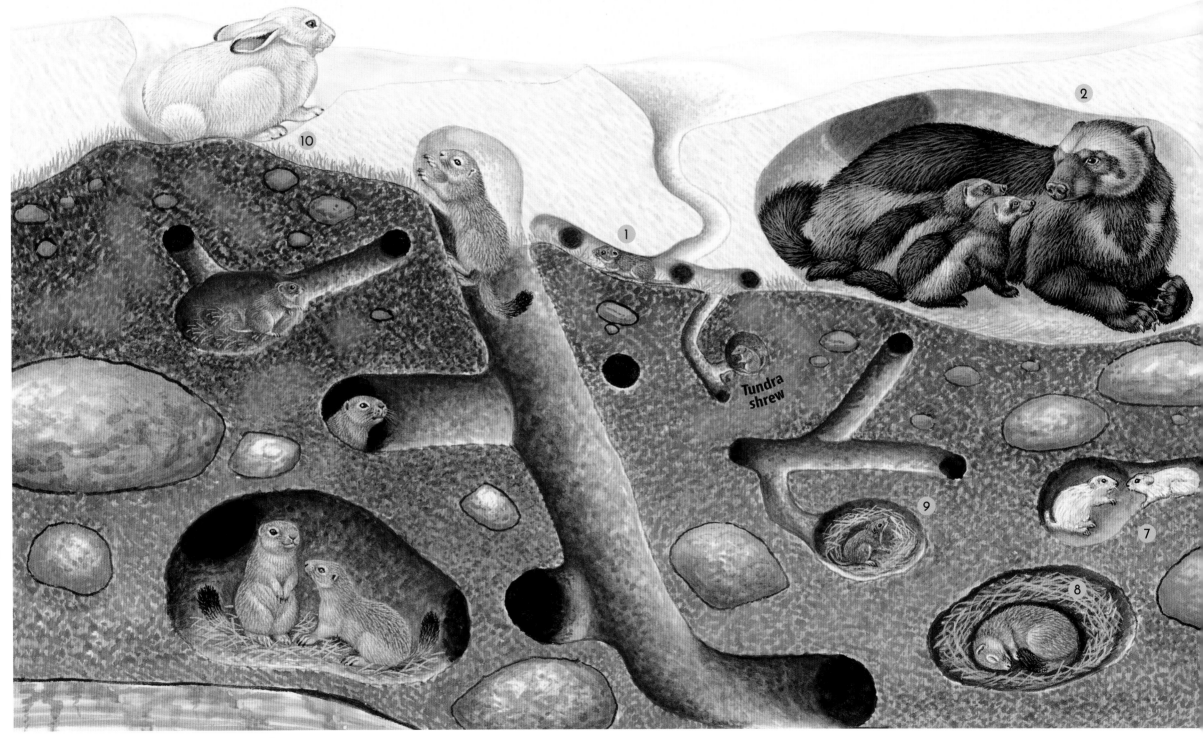

10 With its dense fur, which turns white in winter, the *Arctic hare* is well adapted to life in the cold. When not feeding, it burrows into snowdrifts to keep warm.

Tundra shrew

9 The *tundra shrew* digs through the earth to find small animals, such as insects and worms, and makes an underground breeding nest.

8 The *Arctic ground squirrel* sleeps in a burrow lined with leaves, grasses, and animal hair. In winter, it can hibernate for up to eight months.

3 With its acute hearing, a *snowy owl* can target lemmings and other small animals even when they are hidden beneath deep snow.

4 *Arctic foxes* often make dens in the stony debris dumped by melting glaciers. This one makes an ideal home for a mother nursing three cubs.

Snowy owls are covered in dense layers of feathers, even on their toes, to keep warm.

5 Like all Arctic voles and lemmings, the *tundra vole* is active all year round. It tunnels through snow or dense grass and stores food in burrows.

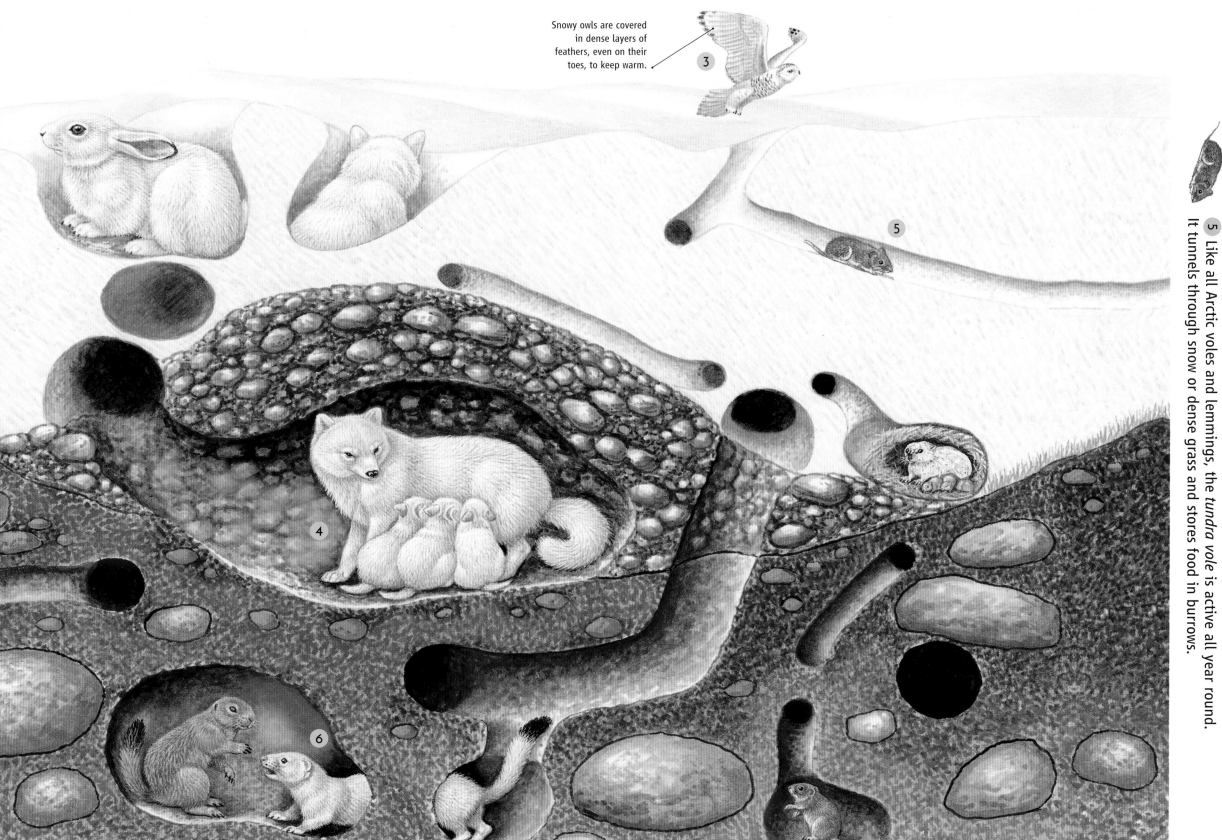

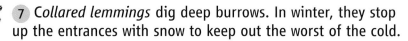

7 C*ollared lemmings* dig deep burrows. In winter, they stop up the entrances with snow to keep out the worst of the cold.

6 The *ermine's* slim body is adapted for hunting other animals in their burrows. Like the fox and hare, it is still in its white winter coat.

GRASSLAND BURROWERS

Out on the broad, open grassy plains of the world, there is nowhere to hide from enemies except below ground. So a wide variety of animals have become expert burrowers, including insects, reptiles, small mammals, and even birds. But some of these animals are not safe, even in their burrows, because many of their enemies can burrow, too.

KEY

Grassland

Where in the world?

Natural grasslands occur in temperate and tropical regions wherever there is enough rain for plants to grow, but not enough for trees to take over and form forests.

Marbled polecat

This strikingly marked hunter lives on the central Asian grasslands known as the steppes. It preys on other burrowers, including hamsters and ground squirrels, and often takes over their burrows instead of digging its own.

North American prairie

The open prairies of central North America offer nowhere to hide from predators. Big grazing animals such as bison and pronghorn rely on their strength and speed, but smaller animals burrow into the ground, as you can see when you turn the page.

Northern pocket gopher

Using their long front claws and big front teeth, pocket gophers dig deep burrows in the soil of the North American prairie. They live almost entirely underground, storing food there to see them through the winter.

Prairie falcon

American bison

Pronghorn

Black-tailed prairie dog

Prairie chicken

A mole snake coils around its prey and squeezes tighter until its victim cannot breathe.

Mole snake

In southern Africa, the mole snake preys on a variety of burrowing grassland animals, especially golden moles. It spends most of its time out of sight below ground.

Golden moles burrow beneath African grasslands to find insects and worms.

Pink fairy armadillo

The smallest of the armadillos, the pink fairy armadillo uses its large front claws to burrow beneath the dry grasslands of central Argentina like a mole. It eats insects, especially ants, finding most of its prey underground.

Hairy-nosed wombat

In Australia, hairy-nosed wombats dig deep burrows that are often shared with other wombats. They sleep in the burrows by day and emerge in the cool of the evening to feed on grass and other plants.

Mara

Big, long-legged relatives of guinea pigs, maras live in groups on South American grasslands called pampas. All the young in a group are cared for by one pair of adults. If danger threatens, they all shelter in the same burrow.

The bobcat is an expert at ambushing small animals such as black-tailed prairie dogs.

Bobcat

Coyote

A prairie dog watches for danger from the mound that forms the rim of its burrow entrance.

A deadly enemy of small mammals, the *prairie rattlesnake* is equipped to locate them in their dark burrows, kill them, and swallow them whole.

The *hispid pocket mouse* gets its name from its two cheek pouches, which it uses to carry seeds and other food back to its burrow.

NORTH AMERICAN PRAIRIE
A hidden city beneath the ground

In places where wild prairie grassland still survives, the ground beneath the hooves of grazing bison is often honeycombed with the burrow networks of prairie dogs. Some of these are adopted by different animals, including the prairie dog's enemies, but other animals dig their own.

Notorious for the foul smell it produces if attacked, the *striped skunk* uses a burrow as a nursery den.

Unlike the prairie dog, the *thirteen-lined ground squirrel* usually lives alone in a burrow it digs itself.

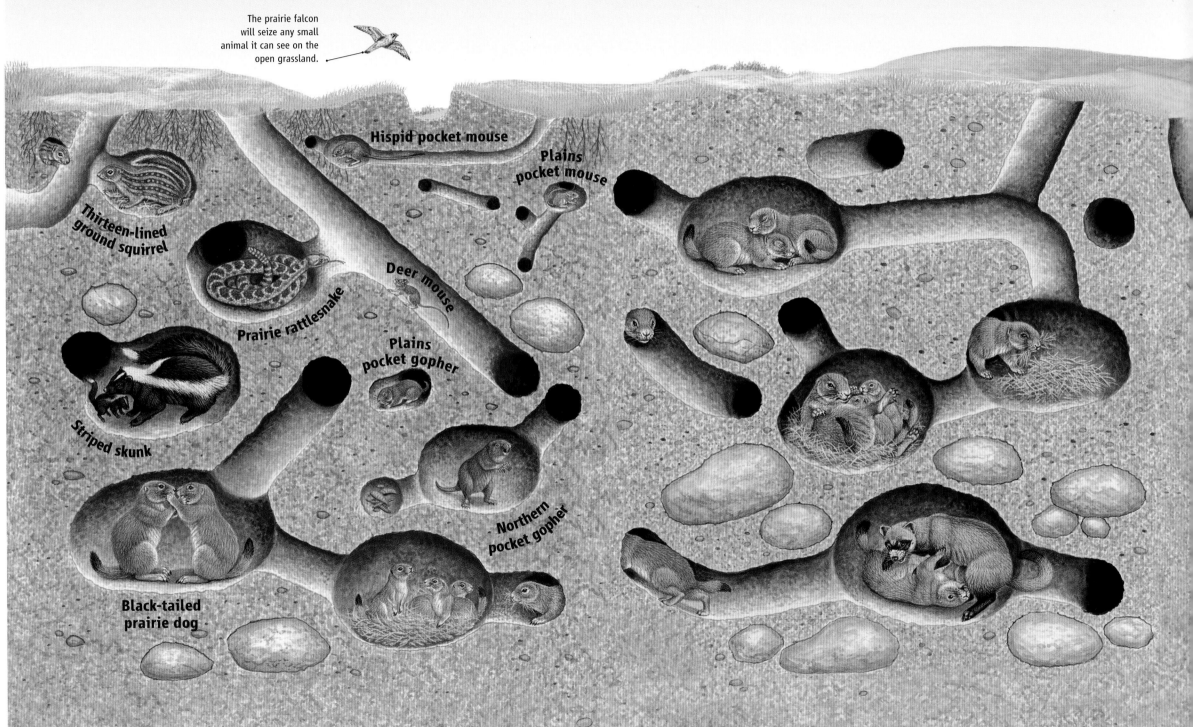

The prairie falcon will seize any small animal it can see on the open grassland.

Hispid pocket mouse

Plains pocket mouse

Thirteen-lined ground squirrel

Deer mouse

Prairie rattlesnake

Plains pocket gopher

Striped skunk

Northern pocket gopher

Black-tailed prairie dog

A type of ground squirrel, the *black-tailed prairie dog* lives in big colonies that excavate huge burrow networks known as prairie dog towns.

Now very rare, the *black-footed ferret* specializes in hunting prairie dogs. It also uses their burrows for resting and rearing its young.

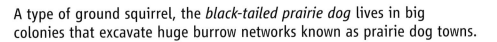

Living in a region with no trees, *burrowing owls* nest in burrows. They nearly always use those of small mammals such as prairie dogs.

 An old badger hole makes a perfect den for a *bobcat*, which usually lies low by day and emerges in the evening to hunt animals like this rabbit.

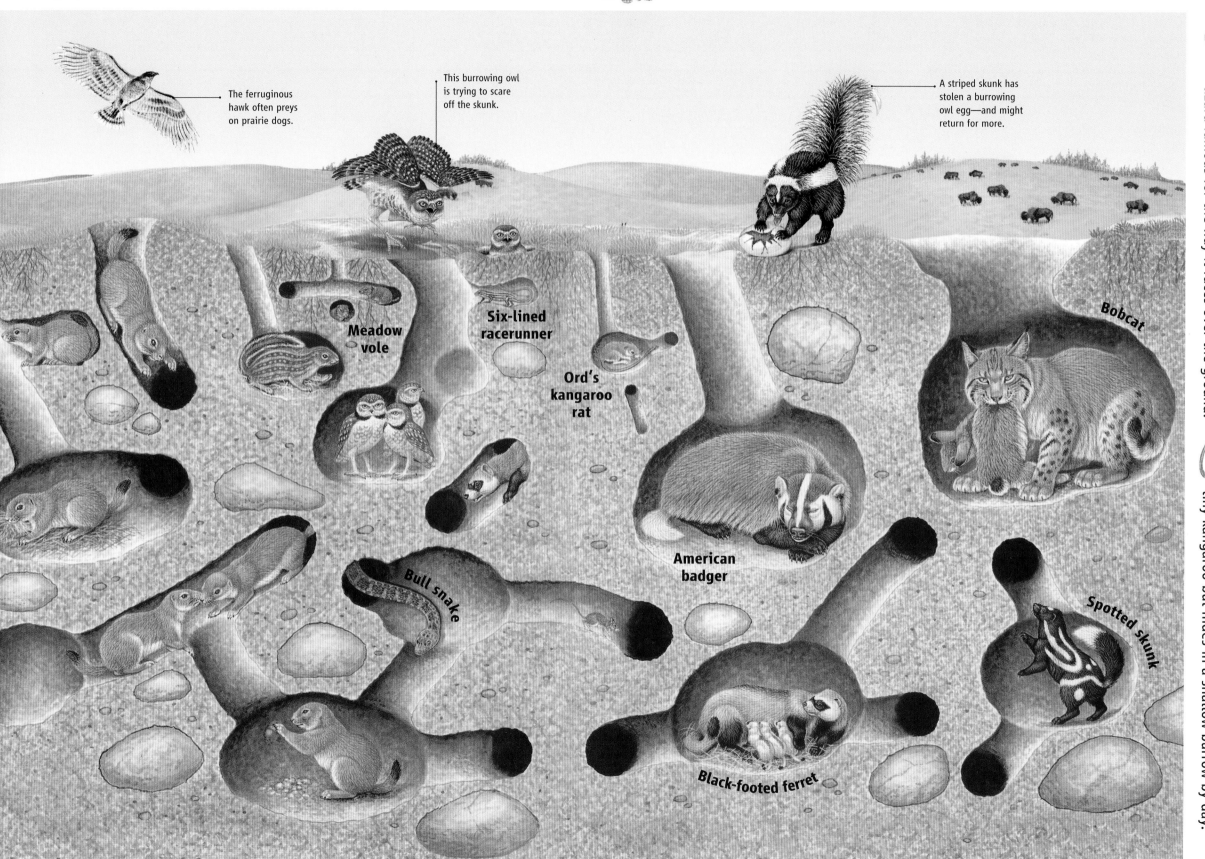

The ferruginous hawk often preys on prairie dogs.

This burrowing owl is trying to scare off the skunk.

A striped skunk has stolen a burrowing owl egg—and might return for more.

Meadow vole

Six-lined racerunner

Ord's kangaroo rat

Bobcat

Bull snake

American badger

Spotted skunk

Black-footed ferret

The sleek *six-lined racerunner* is an insect-eating lizard famous for the way it races over the ground.

Ord's kangaroo rat hops on its long hind legs like a tiny kangaroo but hides in a shallow burrow by day.

The *bull snake* slips into burrows to find ground squirrels and similar prey, seizing them and squeezing them to death like a boa constrictor.

 One of the biggest burrowers, the *American badger* preys on other burrowing animals and will even tackle highly venomous rattlesnakes.

DESERT BURROWERS

Most deserts are burning hot during the day but cold at night. All over the world, many desert animals dig burrows to shelter from the daytime heat and emerge after dark when it is cooler to forage for food.

KEY

Desert

Where in the world?

Deserts are places that get very little rain. Most of them lie in the warm subtropical zones to the north and south of the wet, steamy tropical rainforests.

Termite hunter

Tiny insects called termites build towerlike nest mounds out of desert soil cemented together with their saliva. The nest provides shelter from the desert heat, but a hungry aardvark can break into the mound with its claws and scoop up hundreds of termites with its long, sticky tongue.

Darkling beetle

The darkling beetles that live in deserts escape the heat and their enemies by hiding underground, but do not dig proper burrows. They just dive into the sand headfirst, wriggling from side to side until they are safely buried.

Desert tortoises often feed on the juicy cacti that grow in American deserts.

Desert tortoise

The American desert tortoise controls its body temperature by spending a lot of time in a deep burrow, which it digs with its strong front legs.

Monitor

The Australian short-tailed pygmy monitor hunts by day but often hides in a burrow to avoid being eaten by larger lizards.

African desert

Many animals live in this southwest African desert. Turn the page to see which creatures have retreated underground to stay cool.

A single termite mound can be home to up to 2 million termites. A simple air-conditioning system keeps the air inside the nest cooler than its surroundings.

Rock hyrax

Namaqua sandgrouse

Yellow mongoose

Spotted hyena

Springbok

Hunting dogs

Warthog

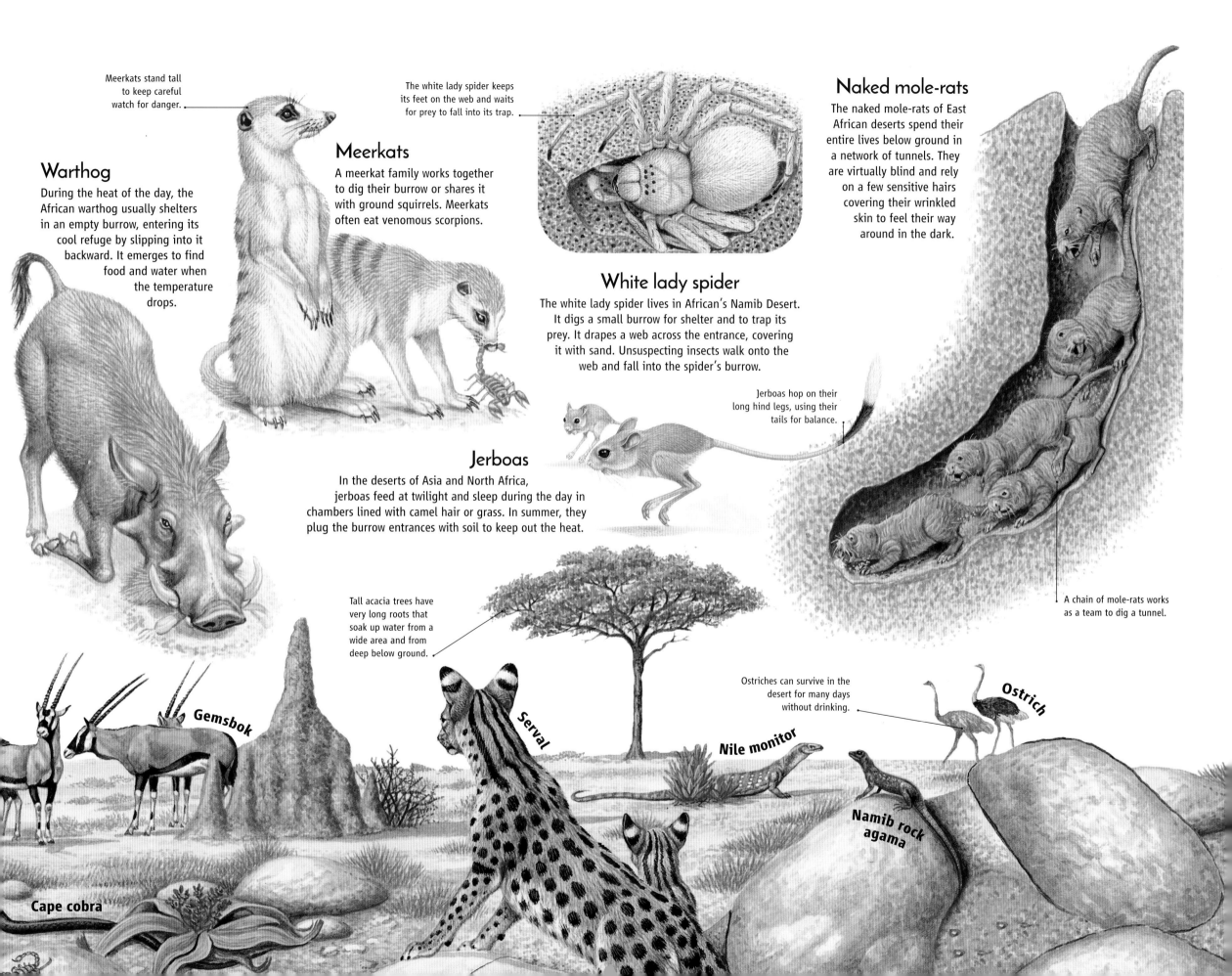

Meerkats stand tall to keep careful watch for danger.

The white lady spider keeps its feet on the web and waits for prey to fall into its trap.

Naked mole-rats

The naked mole-rats of East African deserts spend their entire lives below ground in a network of tunnels. They are virtually blind and rely on a few sensitive hairs covering their wrinkled skin to feel their way around in the dark.

Warthog

During the heat of the day, the African warthog usually shelters in an empty burrow, entering its cool refuge by slipping into it backward. It emerges to find food and water when the temperature drops.

Meerkats

A meerkat family works together to dig their burrow or shares it with ground squirrels. Meerkats often eat venomous scorpions.

White lady spider

The white lady spider lives in African's Namib Desert. It digs a small burrow for shelter and to trap its prey. It drapes a web across the entrance, covering it with sand. Unsuspecting insects walk onto the web and fall into the spider's burrow.

Jerboas hop on their long hind legs, using their tails for balance.

Jerboas

In the deserts of Asia and North Africa, jerboas feed at twilight and sleep during the day in chambers lined with camel hair or grass. In summer, they plug the burrow entrances with soil to keep out the heat.

A chain of mole-rats works as a team to dig a tunnel.

Tall acacia trees have very long roots that soak up water from a wide area and from deep below ground.

Ostriches can survive in the desert for many days without drinking.

Gemsbok

Serval

Nile monitor

Ostrich

Namib rock agama

Cape cobra

African ground squirrels dig tunnels with their sharp claws. They can close their nostrils to stop loose soil from getting in.

The venomous *Cape cobra* will eat any animal that it can catch and swallow whole, even pursuing prey such as gerbils into their burrows.

AFRICAN DESERT
Hiding from the scorching Sun

Some hot deserts are vast expanses of sand, but others, like this one in southwest Africa, are rocky and dotted with hardy plants that are able to survive long droughts. The plants support a variety of animals adapted to cope with the harsh climate.

The walls of the mound are made by termites working together. Each insect makes its own mini bricks by chewing earth and mixing it with saliva. This makes tiny pellets that are pushed onto the walls where they dry hard.

The queen termite's enlarged white abdomen is full of eggs. She can lay thousands of eggs in a day.

Termites chew up leaves and store them in the nest where they compost into food.

The scaly *ground pangolin* lives in a burrow abandoned by another animal or digs one itself. It hunts ants and termites at night, scooping them up with its amazingly long tongue.

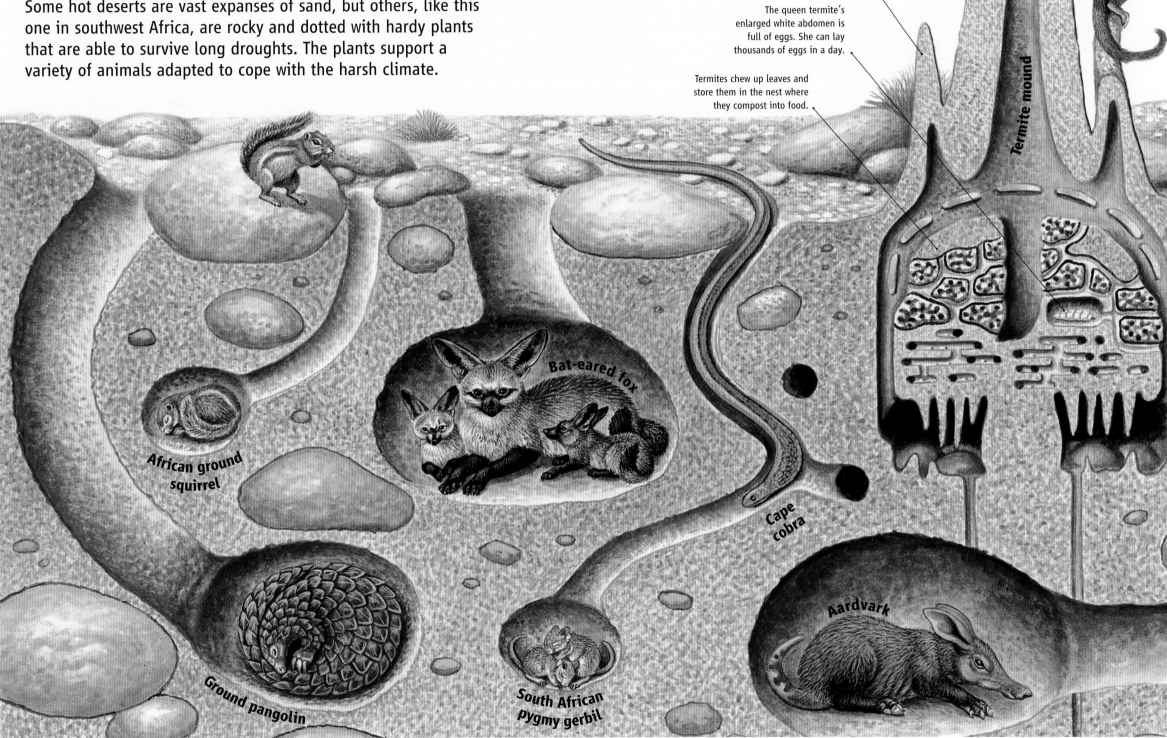

Termite mound

Bat-eared fox

African ground squirrel

Cape cobra

Aardvark

Ground pangolin

South African pygmy gerbil

A *South African pygmy gerbil* lives in a maze of small tunnels. It has many predators, so it is always on the lookout for danger.

Related to the meerkat, the *yellow mongoose* lives in burrows in groups of up to 20. It hunts insects and other small animals.

A *thick-tailed scorpion* seizes prey with its pincers before killing it with the powerful sting in its tail.

The *serval* hunts mainly by sound, using its big, mobile ears to detect and pinpoint the slightest rustle of prey in the dry desert vegetation.

An aardvark usually spends the entire day hidden underground in its network of burrows. It emerges into the open after sunset to search for its ant and termite prey.

The welwitschia can live for more than 1,000 years. Its leaves can grow to 13 feet (4 meters) long and help it absorb moisture from fog.

Vividly colored males perch on sun-baked rocks to display to their rivals.

Namib rock agama

Thick-tailed scorpion

Yellow mongoose

Serval

Cape mole-rat

Springhare

A *springhare* digs a burrow with a side tunnel to escape from predators. It sleeps on its haunches with its tail tucked between its legs.

 Using its big, flattened front claws as spades, the *aardvark* is a fast, powerful digger. It can dig tunnels up to 43 feet (13 meters) long.

 Cape mole-rats live almost entirely underground. They use their chisel-like teeth to loosen the soil before kicking it out of the tunnel.

FRESHWATER BURROWERS

Many animals burrow into the soft banks of lakes, rivers, and streams—especially those that find their food in the water. A waterside burrow makes an ideal nesting site for a kingfisher and a perfect nursery for an otter. A family of beavers will even create their own pond, which surrounds their home and keeps them safe from their enemies.

Nesting kingfishers

In spring, pairs of common kingfishers dig burrows in steep riverbanks. Each burrow is up to 3 feet (90 centimeters) long, sloping upward, and ending in a nesting chamber where the female lays up to seven glossy white eggs.

When the young hatch, both parents must work hard to catch food and bring it back to the nest.

Here, the adult male—on the left—is feeding an almost fully grown chick inside the burrow.

Otter families

For this Asian small-clawed otter and her well-grown young, their riverbank burrow offers easy access to the water where they hunt for fish, frogs, and other prey. The burrow can be home for up to seven pups and their parents.

Adult otters gather grass to make a comfortable nest in their nursery den.

Duck-billed platypus

The extraordinary egg-laying platypus hunts small animals in eastern Australian rivers. It rests and raises its young in riverside burrows that can be up to 66 feet (20 meters) long.

Walls waterproofed with mud and clay

Belted kingfisher

Webbed feet

Branch gnawed off a felled tree

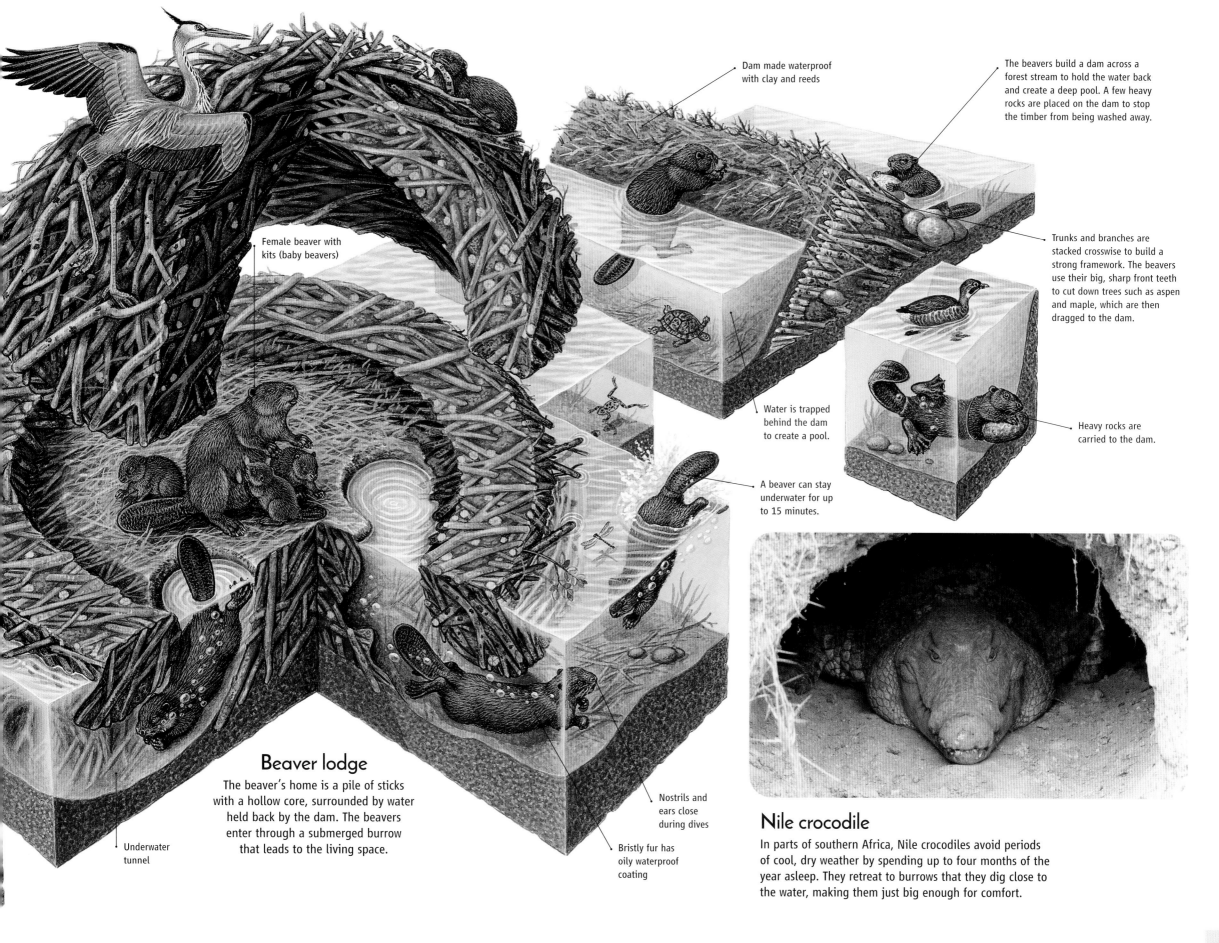

Dam made waterproof with clay and reeds

The beavers build a dam across a forest stream to hold the water back and create a deep pool. A few heavy rocks are placed on the dam to stop the timber from being washed away.

Trunks and branches are stacked crosswise to build a strong framework. The beavers use their big, sharp front teeth to cut down trees such as aspen and maple, which are then dragged to the dam.

Female beaver with kits (baby beavers)

Water is trapped behind the dam to create a pool.

Heavy rocks are carried to the dam.

A beaver can stay underwater for up to 15 minutes.

Beaver lodge

The beaver's home is a pile of sticks with a hollow core, surrounded by water held back by the dam. The beavers enter through a submerged burrow that leads to the living space.

Underwater tunnel

Nostrils and ears close during dives

Bristly fur has oily waterproof coating

Nile crocodile

In parts of southern Africa, Nile crocodiles avoid periods of cool, dry weather by spending up to four months of the year asleep. They retreat to burrows that they dig close to the water, making them just big enough for comfort.

GOING UNDERGROUND

Tunneling into the ground can be hard work, so most burrowing animals are equipped with a variety of features such as slender bodies and powerful digging tools that help make it easier. They also have other adaptations to life underground, including special senses that help them find their way in the dark, locate food, or track down prey.

Underground hunter

Mice, voles, and similar small mammals dive into burrows to escape their enemies. But there is no escape from a weasel, which is slim enough to follow them into their tunnels. Many relatives of the weasel, including stoats and polecats, have the same elongated, tunnel-hunting body shape.

A weasel is heavier than its prey and much longer, but its body is just as slender.

Built for tunneling

An African cape mole-rat has a stumpy body, short legs, and tiny ears—all ideal for life in a burrow. It digs with its big front teeth, allowing it to tunnel through harder ground than most burrowers.

The mole-rat's lips can close behind its teeth to stop soil from getting in its mouth.

Common vole

Digging in

A mole digs with its very broad front feet, which are equipped with stout claws and driven by powerful shoulder muscles. As it digs, it pushes soil behind it and out of the tunnel to make molehills.

Bracing itself with its back feet, the mole scrapes at the soil with its claws to loosen it.

The mole forces the soil aside and back down the tunnel, then shuffles forward to dig out some more.

Living in the dark

Specialized for a life spent almost entirely underground, the European mole has huge shovel-like hands for digging and short, velvety, black fur that allows it to move easily forward or backward through its tunnels.

Moles have no visible external ears, just openings hidden beneath their thick fur that enable them to hear low-pitched sounds.

A mole's eyes are tiny, because it has little use for good vision in total darkness.

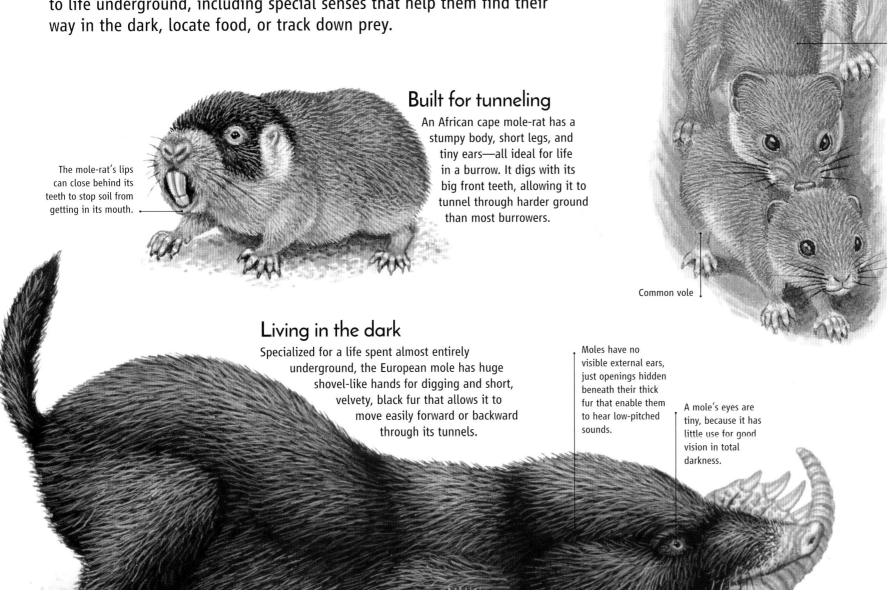

Earthworms are a mole's favorite prey, though it will eat all kinds of small burrowing animals.

Tools for the job

The giant armadillo of South America has enormous, pickaxe-shaped front claws that can be up to 8.7 inches (22 centimeters) long. They make ideal digging tools, both for excavating the armadillo's burrows and for breaking into the hardened mud nests of termites, its main prey.

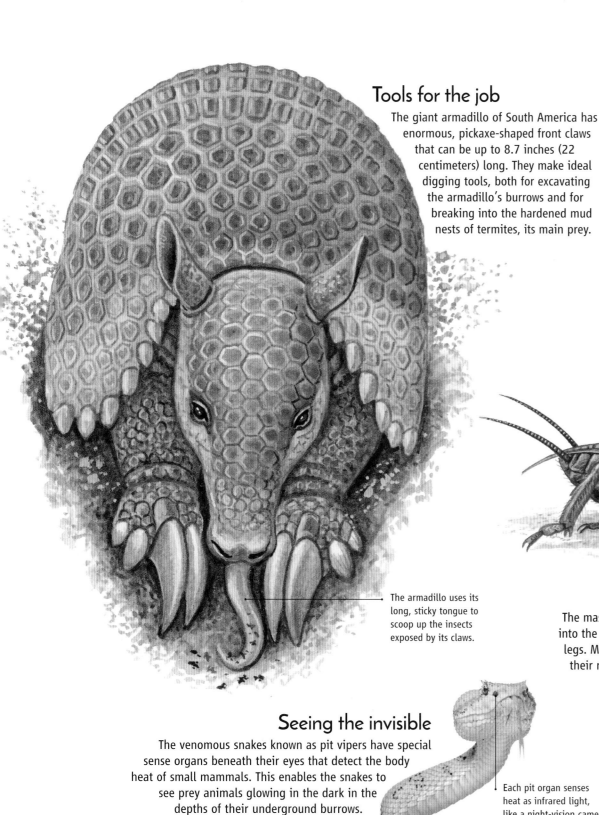

The armadillo uses its long, sticky tongue to scoop up the insects exposed by its claws.

Swimming through sand

A sleek, shiny-skinned lizard, the sandfish skink of North Africa and Arabia owes its name to the way it burrows through dry desert sand. Tucking its short legs close to its body, it wriggles through the sand like a long-bodied fish swimming through water.

Hardened like the claws of a crab, a mole cricket's broad front legs make very efficient spades.

Heavy engineering

The massively built mole cricket is perfectly adapted for digging into the ground, with its armored body and hugely powerful front legs. Male mole crickets dig trumpet-shaped burrows that make their rasping songs sound louder, while females dig to create chambers where they can lay their eggs.

Touch sensitive

Away from the burrow entrance, there is no light at all, so animals cannot use their eyes to navigate. Many mammals such as this rabbit rely on touch, using their highly sensitive whiskers to feel their way through their burrow networks.

Each stiff, wiry whisker is linked to sensory cells that detect every movement.

Seeing the invisible

The venomous snakes known as pit vipers have special sense organs beneath their eyes that detect the body heat of small mammals. This enables the snakes to see prey animals glowing in the dark in the depths of their underground burrows.

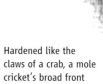

Each pit organ senses heat as infrared light, like a night-vision camera.

Borrowing a burrow

Many animals that use burrows would rather not dig their own. The Atlantic puffin nests in burrows but often adopts the abandoned home of a rabbit. Even so, puffins spend a lot of time cleaning, repairing, and extending their borrowed burrows when they return to land each spring.

BRILLIANT BURROWERS

All kinds of animals from all over the world dig burrows. They range from tiny insects and spiders to relatively big mammals such as badgers. A burrow can be a safe refuge from predators, but for most burrowing animals, it is a comfortable place to sleep, rest, and avoid cold winds or hot sunshine when they are not out in the open looking for food.

The skunk's spray can accurately hit a target more than 10 feet (3 meters) away.

Spotted skunk

Like all skunks, the spotted skunk defends itself by spraying enemies with foul-smelling oily liquid produced by a pair of glands on its bottom. When threatened, it stands on its forefeet and arches the back part of its body forward to take aim.

American badger

The burly American badger is built for digging, with powerful front limbs and strong claws. It spends a lot of its time underground and often chases small burrowing prey, such as this thirteen-lined ground squirrel, into their tunnels.

Ground pangolin

Uniquely among mammals, pangolins are covered with overlapping scales, forming a tough, flexible armor. The African ground pangolin walks on its back feet and uses its front claws to dig for ants and termites.

Spider wasp

There are many types of spider wasps. They hunt spiders, paralyzing them with their stings and dragging them into burrows. The wasp lays an egg on its victim, and when the wasp grub hatches, it eats the spider.

The paralyzed spider is placed in a burrow dug by the spider wasp.

This baby pangolin is saving energy by riding on its mother's tail as she searches for prey.

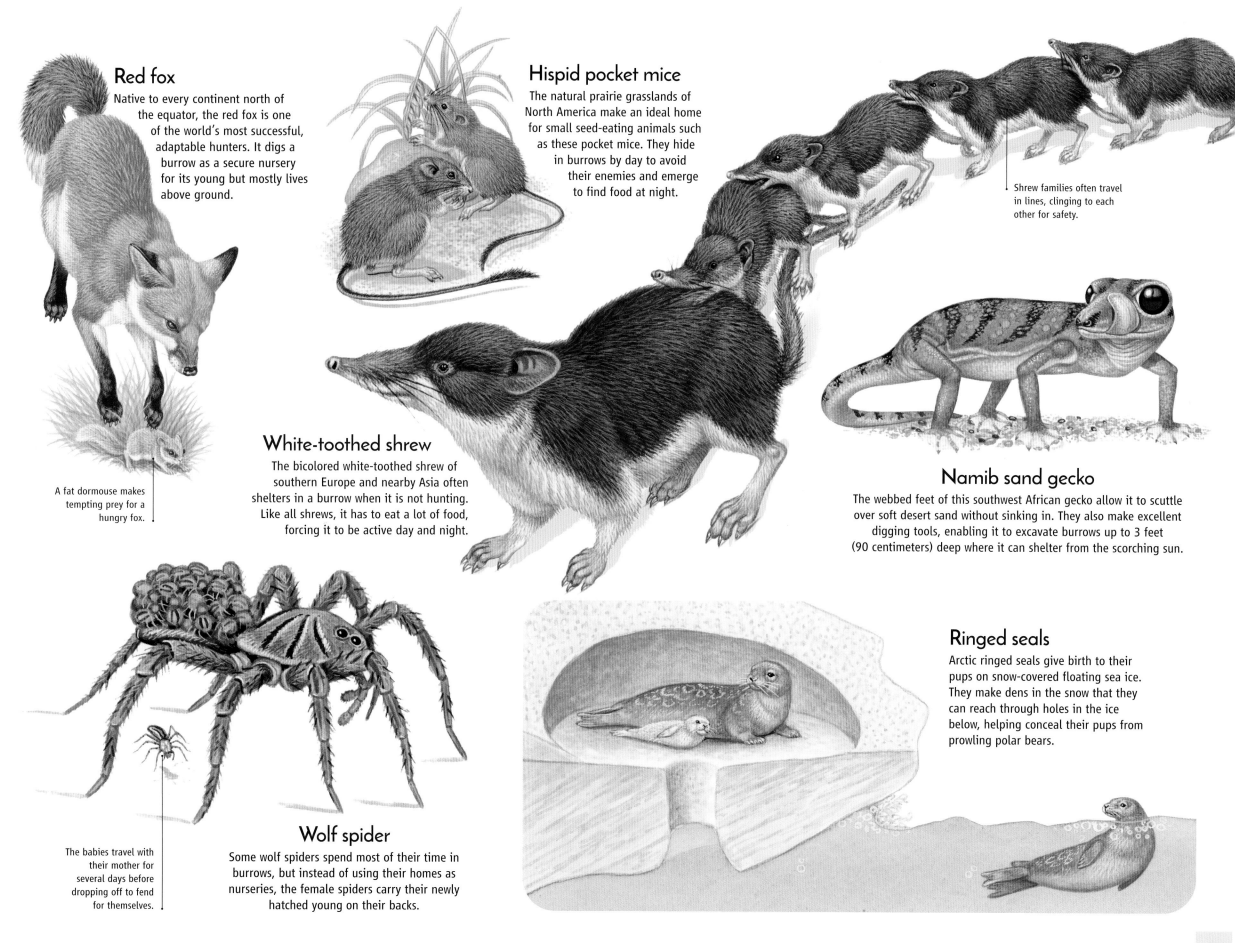

Red fox

Native to every continent north of the equator, the red fox is one of the world's most successful, adaptable hunters. It digs a burrow as a secure nursery for its young but mostly lives above ground.

A fat dormouse makes tempting prey for a hungry fox.

Hispid pocket mice

The natural prairie grasslands of North America make an ideal home for small seed-eating animals such as these pocket mice. They hide in burrows by day to avoid their enemies and emerge to find food at night.

Shrew families often travel in lines, clinging to each other for safety.

White-toothed shrew

The bicolored white-toothed shrew of southern Europe and nearby Asia often shelters in a burrow when it is not hunting. Like all shrews, it has to eat a lot of food, forcing it to be active day and night.

Namib sand gecko

The webbed feet of this southwest African gecko allow it to scuttle over soft desert sand without sinking in. They also make excellent digging tools, enabling it to excavate burrows up to 3 feet (90 centimeters) deep where it can shelter from the scorching sun.

Wolf spider

Some wolf spiders spend most of their time in burrows, but instead of using their homes as nurseries, the female spiders carry their newly hatched young on their backs.

The babies travel with their mother for several days before dropping off to fend for themselves.

Ringed seals

Arctic ringed seals give birth to their pups on snow-covered floating sea ice. They make dens in the snow that they can reach through holes in the ice below, helping conceal their pups from prowling polar bears.

GLOSSARY

adaptation
The way in which an animal changes its body or behavior to survive in its habitat.

ambush
A surprise attack made by an animal from a hiding place.

armored
To have a naturally hard body covering that provides protection.

bolt-hole
A safe place to escape to when in danger.

camouflage
Colors or markings on an animal that match its surroundings, helping it hide.

climate
The average weather in a particular area over a long period of time.

colony
Animals that live closely together in a group.

deciduous tree
A deciduous tree sheds its leaves in winter.

Pygmy gerbil

drought
A long period of time without rain.

dung
The natural waste of animals.

equator
An imaginary line around the middle of Earth that lies at an equal distance from the Earth's poles.

forage
To wander in search of food.

fungus
A type of living thing that is neither a plant nor an animal and feeds on living or dead organisms.

habitat
The natural home of an animal.

hibernation
To spend the winter months in a deep sleep.

mammal
A warm-blooded animal that feeds its young on milk produced by the female.

migration
The seasonal movement of animals to and from breeding or feeding grounds.

predator
An animal that hunts another animal to kill and eat it.

European badger

prey
An animal that is, or could be, killed and eaten by another animal.

sap
The watery fluid that is carried inside plants to provide nourishment.

temperate
An area or climate with temperatures that are not too hot or too cold.

tropical
An area or climate around the equator with hot temperatures and high rainfall.

venomous
Describes an animal that can inject a poisonous substance through a bite or sting.

whiskers
Stiff, sensitive hairs sprouting from a mammal's face.

Index

ACKNOWLEDGMENTS

Dorling Kindersley would like to thank: **Illustrator** Richard Orr, courtesy of Bernard Thornton Artists, Mallorca; **Creative retouching** Steve Crozier; **Proofreader** Hazel Beynon; **Indexer** Elizabeth Wise

The publisher would also like to thank the following for their kind permission to reproduce their images: 4 Dreamstime.com: Michele Cornelius (tr). **Getty Images / iStock:** abriendomundo (br); E+ / Onfokus (cra); Danielrao (crb). **5 Alamy Stock Photo:** kevin hellon (cra). **Dreamstime.com:** Ecophoto (bc); Andrew Roland (tc). **Getty Images / iStock:** Christopher Smith (crb). **14 Alamy Stock Photo:** imageBROKER / Frank Sommariva (tr). **26 Alamy Stock Photo:** agefotostock / Michiel Andreas Klootwijk (bl); Soumyajit Nandy (cla); blickwinkel / D. Mahlke (tc); David Boag (tr). **naturepl.com:** D. Parer & E. Parer-Cook (crb). **27 Alamy Stock Photo:** Nick Greaves; Agfa Awards Winner (br). **29 Alamy Stock Photo:** David Chapman (br); Chris Mattison (tc). **Dreamstime.com:** Isselee (bl).

All other images © Dorling Kindersley
For further information see: www.dkimages.com